BOSTON

A Picture Book to Remember Her by

CRESCENT BOOKS
NEW YORK

CLB 991
© 1987 Illustrations and text: Colour Library Books Ltd.
     Guildford, Surrey, England.
Text filmsetting by Acesetters Ltd., Richmond, Surrey, England.
Printed and bound in Barcelona, Spain by Cronion, S.A.
1987 edition published by Crescent Books, distributed by Crown Publishers, Inc.
ISBN 0 517 288613
h g f e d c b a

Boston was founded to be the center of a new society in a promised land. The English Puritans with whom the city began in 1630 came in search of freedom to practise their non-conformist religion, away from a repressive Church of England. The Puritans were mostly merchants, professionals and yeoman farmers – the new "middle-class" – who had attained to a level of wealth and education, but still could have no respected and responsible place within the jealously guarded established order.

The immediate impetus for the founding of Boston came with the creation of the Massachusetts Bay Company. A royal charter was granted to a group of Puritan leaders, under the headship of John Winthrop, who agreed to go to New England and fulfill the mercantile purpose of the charter provided that the charter and the government of the settlement be given over entirely to the settlers. This arrangement gave them the freedom to set up and sustain their new society, the main town of which became the seaport of Boston.

The Puritan cause met with political success in England too, with the overthrow of Charles I, and his execution in 1649. With the setting up of the Commonwealth under Cromwell the morals and politics of the mother country and her independently-minded colony were in complete sympathy, and personal and trade links between Boston and London were strong.

In 1660 the old order was returned with a vengeance with the restoration of Charles II to the throne of England. Government structured upon rigid Puritan principles relaxed into the considerably looser morals of the ruler by birthright. London and Boston were no longer of one mind, though it was not until 1684 that the former sought to impose its governing will. The charter of the Massachussetts Bay Company was declared void in that year, and royal authority vested in Sir Edmund Andros as New England's first governor in 1686.

Two years later Charles II's successor, James II, was deposed in the Glorious Revolution which put the protestant William of Orange on the throne. In celebration, the people of Boston deposed and imprisoned their high-handed royal governor. The campaign of words that followed secured them a new, reforming charter which, notably, ended the requirement that a man had to be a Church of England member in order to vote. However, it failed to return power to a "civil Body Politick" of Bostonians, and a new royal governor was appointed.

By 1700, Boston's seagoing fleet, on which her prosperity was based, had expanded to become second only to those of London and Bristol in the English-speaking world. The center of the thriving province of New England, Boston was now competing with the mother country in trade, fishing and manufacturing. On realizing this untoward threat, the government of George III sought to reverse the trend towards independence and recoup its rightful due by heavy restrictions on trade – the city's lifeblood.

The new political ideals bred by the enlightenment – the questioning of the divine right of kings, and the seeds of democracy – had long been in the minds of New Englanders, though aversion to British sovereignty on moral grounds had mellowed since the days of the founding Puritans. Now, however, both their freedom and their material prosperity were endangered, and when to these initial measures were added ever more restrictive, autocratic demands, Bostonian indignation was roused to a sufficient pitch to spark the Revolution. In 1765 the passing of the Stamp Act led to riot and the burning of the governor's house. In rapid succession the Townshend Acts (1767), Tea Act (1773) and Intolerable Acts (1774) heightened the disaffection. The Tea Act was followed by the famed Boston Tea Party, at which colonists, disguised as Indians, deposited three shiploads of tea in the harbor.

On April 19, 1775 shots were exchanged at Lexington and Concord. During the winter of 1776 General Washington's Continental Army besieged the British in Boston and, on March 17, 1776 the royal governor, the British troops and loyalist civilians were forced to abandon the town.

The American Revolution officially ended in 1783 with the Treaty of Paris. Before this, in 1780, Boston had reassumed control of its own affairs in orderly fashion with the framing of a democratic constitution. The Puritans' intentions of independence from a morally and politically unacceptable authority were fulfilled, though the new society which regained that independence was rapidly becoming far-removed from their rigid design.

The town's economy thrived even more with the opening up of lucrative trade routes to China and India, replacing those damaged by the break with England. Large numbers of European immigrants swelled Boston's population, increasing it more than twentyfold during the 19th century. Naturally, these peoples brought with them their respective churches, diversifying the religious life of the city with the teachings of the Roman Catholic church, through Unitarianism, to transcendentalism and Christian Science. The city's cultural outlook was also broadened and enriched and, with the founding of many institutes of learning during the 19th century to add to the 17th century college of Harvard, Boston became known as a place of refinement, scholarship and enlightenment. The people of Boston had attained their long-sought-for freedom – both politically and from any form of religious repression – and in this liberal atmosphere Boston grew into the city of today.

The colorful markets and street vendors of Boston
bring atmosphere and excitement to the city. Above: a
fruit seller tempts passing shoppers with his produce.
Below: a pretzel-seller aims playfully with his sauce
bottle. Right: the many blooms of Quincy Market. Bottom
right: the undercover awnings of Faneuil Hall
Marketplace. Top right: a pagoda-roofed telephone booth
on a corner of Chinatown.

Bottom: the cold snows of winter bring silence and inactivity to the boats of the Charles River which in summer months take to the waters at almost every opportunity (right, below and facing page bottom). Left: the older buildings of Beacon Hill spread beneath the high rise offices of modern Boston.

Top left and main picture: the magnificent, Renaissance-style First Church of Christ, Scientist, the mother church of the Christian Science church. Above, top and far left: the picturesque streets, street lamps and uneven sidewalks of Beacon Hill, long the most prestigious residential area of Boston. Inset left: colorful signs in Chinatown.

Thoughts of Old Boston are evoked by Copp's Hill Burying Ground (above) with ship masts rising behind houses beyond. Right: the Prudential building and John Hancock Tower rise above the city. Bottom right and below: the brick houses of Beacon Hill. Bottom center: the oldest restaurant in Boston.

Top and inset facing page: the House of Representatives, (above) the Senate Chamber and (right) the Memorial Hall, in the State House. Facing page main picture: Boston Public Library. Overleaf: (left) Long Wharf and (right) the Massachusetts Institute of Technology.

The Boston Public Gardens (these pages) lie in the heart of the city. They are famous not only for their flowers and lawns, but also for the swan boats which glide across the lake. Overleaf: (top left) Park Street Church from Boston Common; (bottom left) the banks of the Charles River by Memorial Drive and (right) the Charles River looking towards Harvard University.

These pages: the buildings of Beacon Hill reflect the styles of the late-18th to 19th centuries.

These pages: Quincy Market and Faneuil Hall. Overleaf: two fine aerial views towards the city center from over Harvard University.

Top: the crucifix and altar of Trinity Church. Above: the carved pews of the Old South Church. Right: the great dome of the First Church of Christ, Scientist dominates the older, more modest church before it. Inset top: the Charles Street Meeting House. Inset bottom left: the pulpit and (inset bottom right) the exterior of the Old South Meeting House which was erected in 1729. On December 16, 1773, 5,000 citizens met here to debate the tax on tea prior to engaging in the Boston Tea Party.

Left: the Weeks Memorial Foot Bridge crosses the Charles River. Above: Park Street Church, where William Lloyd Garrison gave an anti-slavery speech in 1829. Below: the Old Corner Bookstore, which has been connected with books since 1712. Top left: Faneuil Hall Marketplace. Bottom left: Back Bay. Overleaf: the skyline of Boston with (bottom left) North Station.

Right and top center: Copp's Hill Burying Ground. Top left: Beacon Hill. Inset top: the statue of George Washington in the Public Gardens (above). Bottom right: Granary Burying Ground. Top right: Old West Church of 1806.

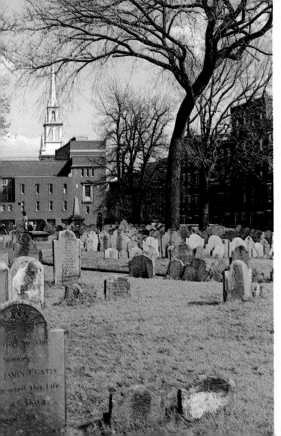

Left: Long Wharf. Above: the frigate *U.S.S. Constitution*, the famous 'Old Ironsides' of the War of 1812. At the Boston Tea Party Museum (top center) the famous event is re-enacted on the *Beaver II* (top right), a replica of one of the ships involved in the original incident.

On June 6th 1968,
Robert Francis Kennedy
was assassinated
in Los Angeles, California.

Left: the elegant and imposing facade of the State House, designed by Charles Bulfinch and completed in 1795. Remaining pictures: scenes from the John F. Kennedy Library which pays tribute to the late President's administration. Overleaf: (bottom center) the *Beaver II* and (remaining pictures) the *U.S.S. Constitution*. The famous old frigate was built in 1797 by Joshua Humphrey but did not see action until 1803. She gained her nickname when in action against the British frigate *HMS Guerriere* she sustained remarkably little damage from the numerous hits received.

Above: a specialist shop on Beacon Hill. Below: the First
Church of Christ, Scientist; the smaller, Romanesque church was
constructed in 1895 and the great domed extension, which is now
used for services, was added in 1903-6. Right and inset top
right: the open space in front of Quincy Market, named for
Josiah Quincy the mayor who conceived the idea of the market
and put it into practice.

Above: the fine statue of
George Washington in the
Public Gardens. Top: the
statue-topped column which
is the Soldiers and Sailors
Monument on Boston Common,
the oldest park in the
nation dating back to 1634.
Right: the distinctive Back
Bay area of the city. The
entire region was reclaimed
at the close of the last
century and its architecture
remains a classic example of
the period.

ROBERT GOULD SHAW

EL OF THE FIFTY FOURTH REGIMENT OF MASSACHUSETTS
RY BORN IN BOSTON OCTOBER X M D CCC XXX
WHILE LEADING THE ASSAULT ON FORT WA
TH CAROLINA JULY XVIII M D CCC XIII

JU

NEW

HERE LIES
THE VOICE

44

Facing page: the monument to Robert Gould Shaw, opposite the State House. Top right: the steps of the State House. Remaining pictures: the Annual Loyalty Day Program, held on May Day on Boston Common.

Below: the City Hall which was designed by Kallmann, McKinnell and Knowles to emphasize the open nature of city government. Above: the city's statue of Paul Revere. Right: the Charles River at Cambridge.

Left: Faneuil Hall, which was given to the city by Peter Faneuil in 1742 to serve as a market. Facing page: the marketplace which lies in front of the hall. Below and bottom: pretzel sellers in the streets of Boston. Overleaf: (left) St. Stephen's and Old North churches from the air and (right) the Larz Anderson Bridge in Cambridge.

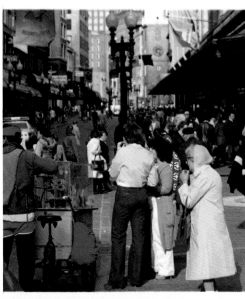

Bottom left: the Museum of Fine Arts on Huntingdon Avenue, which contains one of the most important art collections in the state. Top left: Buckman Tavern in Lexington, where minutemen gathered before fighting the British. Top center: Orchard House, Concord. Left: University Hall, Harvard, built in 1816. Top: the Custom House Tower from Marine Park. Above: the Wayside in Concord.

Above and top: Paul Revere's House, built in 1676 it is restored to Revolutionary condition. Right: Longfellow House, Cambridge. Top center: Paul Revere's statue and St. Stephen's Church. Top right: Old State House.

Left: the russet colors of fall around a house in Duxbury. Remaining pictures: Harvard University is one of the oldest and foremost academic institutions in the States.

of ye Liberty & the Rights of mankind!!!
The Freedom & Independence of America,
sealed & defended with the blood of her sons.

This Monument is erected
By the inhabitants of Lexington,
Under the patronage, & at the expence, of
The Commonwealth of Massachusetts,
To the memory of their Fellow Citizens,
Ensign Robert Munroe, Mess.r Jonas Parker,
Samuel Hadley, Jonathan Harrington Jun.r
Isaac Muzzy, Caleb Harrington and John Brown
Of Lexington, & Asahel Porter of Woburn,
Who fell on this field, the first Victims to the
Sword of British Tyranny & Oppression,
On the morning of the ever memorable
Nineteenth of April, An. Dom. 1775.
The Die was cast!!!
The Blood of these Martyr's,
In the cause of God & their Country,
Was the Cement of the Union of these States, then
Colonies; & gave the spring to the spirit, Firmness
And resolution of their Fellow Citizens.
They rose as one man, to revenge their brethren's
Blood, and at the point of the sword, to assert &
Defend their native Rights.
They nobly dar'd to be free!!
The contest was long, bloody & affecting.
Righteous Heaven approved the solemn appeal;
Victory crowned their arms; and
The Peace, Liberty & Independence of the United
States of America, was their glorious Reward.

Built in the year 1799.

Main picture left: North Bridge,
Concord, where the first skirmish
of the Revolution was fought.
Inset far left: the church on
Lexington Green. Inset left:
Martha Mary's Chapel, Sudbury.
Inset top center: a statue
outside the Museum of Fine Arts.
Top: the Minuteman Statue. Above:
a plaque in Lexington.

Top left: North Bridge in Concord. Above: Lowell House, Harvard University, whose bells came from the Danilov Monastery in Russia complete with a bell-tuner. Left: a fine doorway at Harvard University. Bottom left: a house in Sturbridge.

61

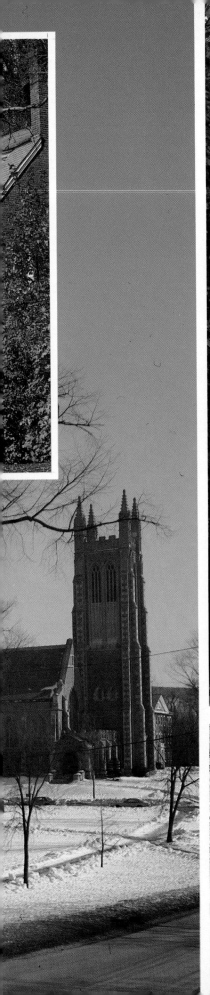

Far left: The First
Congregational Church at
Williamstown. Above: Smith
Halls, Harvard. Overleaf:
the Main Hall of the Museum
of Science.

UNITED STATES

man's first
lunar landing

BANCROFT GALLERY
In Memory of Hugh and Jane Bancroft
Gift of their daughter Mrs. William C. Cox
1977